THEN & NOW

DEAL ISLAND

OPPOSITE: This photograph shows two skipjacks in the Deal Island–Chance Harbor in the 1950s. (Courtesy Jay Harford.)

THEN & NOW

DEAL ISLAND

Claudia Mouery

To all the men and women of the Deal Island / Chance Volunteer Fire Department. All the royalties of this book will go to them. They answer the alarm to protect our homes and families day or night, and many of them are working on the water at sunrise.

Copyright © 2009 by Claudia Mouery
ISBN 978-0-7385-6775-4

Library of Congress Control Number: 2009921047

Published by Arcadia Publishing
Charleston SC, Chicago IL, Portsmouth NH, San Francisco CA

Printed in the United States of America

For all general information contact Arcadia Publishing at:
Telephone 843-853-2070
Fax 843-853-0044
E-mail sales@arcadiapublishing.com
For customer service and orders:
Toll-Free 1-888-313-2665

Visit us on the Internet at www.arcadiapublishing.com

ON THE FRONT COVER: The mid- to late-1930s photograph shows the Wenona Harbor. In the distance are the sail loft to the right and Little Deal Island. At the time of this photograph, there was a sporting lodge on Little Deal Island. The docking area was either soil or covered with oyster shells. The more recent photograph was taken in January 2009. The docking area is now an asphalt parking lot with a public boat ramp. In the background are several soft crab shedding floats and a public restroom. The sail loft is no longer there, and Little Deal Island is no longer inhabitable. The little island is used as a buffer for erosion and was recently reinforced for that purpose. (Then photograph courtesy Charles "Tommy" Northam; now photograph author's collection.)

ON THE BACK COVER: George White delivers ice for the icehouse on Deal Island. Before freezers, everyone used blocks of ice to cool their refrigerators and to keep the catch cold for market. There are two children with White who accompanied him on his deliveries. (Courtesy Albert "Al" Brown.)

CONTENTS

ACKNOWLEDGMENTS

This book is a project of the community; I could never have completed it without their help. Everyone I approached for photographs and the history of the area was helpful. All of the "then" photographs were contributed by residents or past residents of these communities. The information has been gleaned from conversations with neighbors, *The Deal Island Story* by Myra Thomas Long, newspaper articles, and information found in the library in Princess Anne. To my knowledge, none of the photographs violate any copyright law or infringe in any way the literary property of another. All of the "now" photographs were taken by the author.

A special thank-you goes to Albert "Al" Brown and Charles "Tommy" Northam for all the special help they have given me and to my husband of over 40 years, Carl "Bud," for patiently accompanying me throughout the community to gather information and take photographs.

—Claudia A. Mouery

INTRODUCTION

My husband and I moved here after retiring because we found it to be the ideal location for us. Once here, I was surprised to learn there was not very much published about the area. This book is the result of a fund-raiser for the fire company auxiliary. While gathering the information for that project, I realized how much of this area has vanished into history and decided to gather information while there are still people that know the story.

I feel this book will give a glimpse of the independent, self-sustaining community that was once here. I say a glimpse because of the many buildings and businesses of which there are no photographs. The photographs from "then" are old and some in less-than-perfect condition. I have obtained old photographs of many places where now there is nothing but marsh grass, riprap, or open areas to photograph. Many of the existing buildings replaced older structures of which there are no photographs. There were several stores in each of the communities that are no longer in existence, along with a laundromat, crab picking houses, and a crab packing company. I hope you will enjoy this look at days gone by and appreciate the value they have to the families that have lived here for generations.

I learned from some of the reading I have done that Capt. John Smith stopped here while exploring the Chesapeake Bay in 1607. Deal Island was mentioned in Captain Smith's writings as one of his prominent landmarks as he sailed the bay. Several years after Captain Smith returned to England and told of what he found on the bay, three ships made the voyage across the ocean. After an encounter with a bad storm in the bay, two made it to Accomack, Virginia, while the third was driven into Tangier Sound and wrecked. The survivors of that wreck said this land of marsh and wilderness was purgatory, the land of the Devil. Legend says that pirates used "Devil's Island" as their hideout for many years. Eventually Devil's Island was renamed Deal's Island by some religious settlers. Today the "s" has been dropped to make it Deal Island.

If you look at a map of the lower Eastern Shore of Maryland, you will find a place in Somerset County named Deal Island. At first it appears to be just Deal Island, but there are four communities within the island's current boundaries.

Deal Island Road is Route 363 on the map. After traveling about 14 miles west of Maryland Route 13 and crossing a large marsh area, Dames Quarter (originally Damned Quarter) is the first community you will come to, and it is mostly residential. There are two churches, a public boat ramp, and a great place for crabbing without a boat.

After crossing a second marsh area, you enter Chance. There are three churches, two cemeteries, and a convenience store with the only gas pumps in the area other than those found at the docks. In Chance there are two marinas. Windsor Marina, on the south side of Deal Island Road, has boat slips and access to Tangier Sound by way of Deal Island–Chance Harbor. Scott's Cove Marina is the largest marina in the area. Many crab/oyster powerboats and recreational boats berth in this marina. At this time, the skipjack *Kathryn* is also berthed here. This marina may be seen from the bridge and can be accessed on land by traveling through part of the community as well as by boat through the harbor. Scott's Cove Marina is a full-service marina. Repairs for most boat problems, both for powerboats and skipjacks, can be done here.

To get to Deal Island, you must cross a bridge over the harbor. One of four skipjacks often berths here and can usually be seen from the bridge. A public boat ramp is located in the harbor. The entrance to the harbor is just past the bridge on the right. Deal Island Road winds as you travel through the community. This is where many of the community needs are: the firehouse for the Deal Island/Chance Volunteer Fire Department (VFD), the post office for all of the communities, the elementary school, and St. John's Church and cemetery, where the Joshua Thomas Chapel is located.

Deal Island Road continues through the community, winding past homes and some more marsh. Nearest the Chesapeake Bay is the community of Wenona. This was once a very busy fishing village. A large fleet of skipjacks called this harbor home. Today it is still a busy harbor with charter boats and powered oyster/crab boats as well as a convenience store, a small condominium community, a cemetery, and two churches. Deal Island Road comes to an end at the harbor in Wenona. Usually two of the remaining skipjacks will be here.

The area is blessed with many species of birds and wildlife. Be sure to have a camera with you to take shots of the peaceful beauty. You may catch an osprey, pelican, egrets, or snowy egrets if the season is right. The great blue heron and a variety of gulls are here all year long. Occasionally you may get a glimpse of a bald eagle; there are nesting pairs in the area. When you come here, if you stay for a while, you will recognize you are standing with one foot in today and the other in a place of a time long ago.

CHAPTER 1

DAMES QUARTER

The Shores family's country store and post office was in the first community that is now Deal Island. Dames Quarter is approximately 14 miles west of Maryland Route 13. (Courtesy Ruth McInturff.)

On the road leading into Dames Quarter is a very large marsh. There was once a hunting lodge here with a small cottage. Dr. George C. Buzby, grandson of owner George Buzby, is pictured in June 1950. This lodge no longer exists. The photograph above shows a sign and entrance to the Deal Island Wildlife Management Area Wildlife Division, which leads into the marsh where the lodge once was. This wildlife management area is a part of the Maryland Department of Natural Resources (DNR) Land and Water Conservation Project. There is a small boat ramp at the end of the road that is said to be a good fishing spot. The road is very narrow and rutted with thick marsh on both sides, and sometimes the DNR will close the gate to any traffic. (Courtesy Ruth McInturff.)

Some neighbors use a mule to help pull the car that is stuck in the mud and the ditch on the side of the road. This is an example of the muddy road conditions that were normal when this photograph was taken. The road traveled now is not only sturdy blacktop but is also elevated. This helps to stall flooding under normal conditions. Occasionally, when a bad storm arrives or if high tide is exceptionally high, even this road may be under some water for a short time. (Courtesy Ruth McInturff.)

From 1952 until 1982, Henry's Beach was a popular day resort for African Americans and the general public. This was the only resort of this kind in the state of Maryland. It was owned by Lorraine Henry and her husband, George. Families came here to enjoy ball games, bathing, fishing, crabbing, and home-style cooking as well as the black entertainers and musicians of the period. This is a wide view of the original buildings on the property. Now the property is privately owned and is a family home. The location of the buildings is very similar, but there are less buildings and the trees are much taller now. (Courtesy Lorraine Henry.)

Henry's Beach had a restaurant and changing rooms for the patrons. People came here from many areas. Some came on buses for a full day at the beach. The building is still in the same place, but it is no longer a restaurant. It is now a garage, workshop, and storage area for the owners. (Courtesy Lorraine Henry.)

The beach itself at Henry's Beach was a beautiful stretch of sandy waterfront for bathers and those that wished to fish for a while or just relax in the warmth of the sun and feel the breeze from Tangier Sound. Years of erosion have wiped away the lovely beach. Now a sturdy stone wall prevents more erosion, but this is still a lovely place to enjoy the beauty of the area. (Courtesy Lorraine Henry.)

The very popular Henry's Beach had a baseball field that was used by many traveling and local baseball teams, both African American teams and any others that wanted to play there.

A plaque honoring Henry's Beach by Maryland Historical Trust stands beside Deal Island Road in Dames Quarter. (Courtesy Lorraine Henry.)

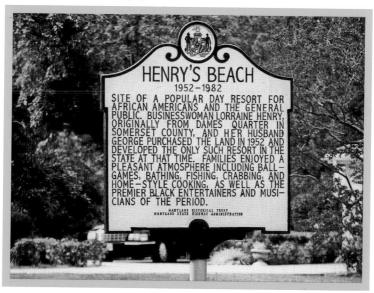

HENRY'S BEACH
1952–1982
SITE OF A POPULAR DAY RESORT FOR AFRICAN AMERICANS AND THE GENERAL PUBLIC. BUSINESSWOMAN LORRAINE HENRY, ORIGINALLY FROM DAMES QUARTER IN SOMERSET COUNTY, AND HER HUSBAND GEORGE PURCHASED THE LAND IN 1952 AND DEVELOPED THE ONLY SUCH RESORT IN THE STATE AT THAT TIME. FAMILIES ENJOYED A PLEASANT ATMOSPHERE INCLUDING BALL–GAMES, BATHING, FISHING, CRABBING, AND HOME–STYLE COOKING, AS WELL AS THE PREMIER BLACK ENTERTAINERS AND MUSI–CIANS OF THE PERIOD.

MARYLAND HISTORICAL TRUST
MARYLAND STATE HIGHWAY ADMINISTRATION

Great Shoals Light was a screw-pile lighthouse in the Chesapeake Bay at the mouth of the Wicomico River. This light was constructed to mark a narrow channel at the entrance to the Wicomico River, as requested by the Maryland General Assembly in 1882. An appropriation was not made until the following year, and further delays pushed the commissioning date to August 1884. In 1966, the light was dismantled and a modern automated light was erected on the old foundation. Several years ago the bell was removed, and it has not been returned. (Courtesy Aileen Webster.)

On June 29, 1983, the Dames Quarter Post Office celebrated 125 years of service with this envelope. The envelope depicts a 1953 photograph of the previous post office and has an insert listing all the postmasters since its establishment on June 29, 1858. During the 1980s, each community had its own post office and its own zip code. This post office was a part of a locally owned convenience store. Some of the post offices were in people's homes. Today there is one post office that services all of the Deal Island communities, and they all have the same zip code. (Courtesy Ruth McInturff.)

125th ANNIVERSARY
Dames Quarter, Md. Post Office
June 29, 1858 - June 29, 1983

Dames Quarter Methodist Church was built in 1854, remodeled in 1916, and burned to the ground during a storm in 1957. The church and all its contents were lost in the fire. The church was rebuilt in 1959 and was dedicated debt free in 1962. When it was dedicated, it was renamed Somerset United Methodist Church. (Courtesy Ruth McInturff.)

Hodson White's school bus transported children to and from school in the 1940s. During the summer, the body of the school bus would be propped on barrels, and a truck body was put on the same frame. The truck, partially seen on the left of the photograph, was used to haul vegetable crops to market. Today a nice bright yellow school bus transports the children to school. (Courtesy Thomas White, son of Hodson White.)

This is the Whites' farmhouse in the 1940s, when the land was farmed and the bus took the children to school. The farm is now a vacation retreat and has been updated and remodeled to accommodate visitors. (Then photograph courtesy Thomas White; postcard courtesy Nancy Goldsmith.)

The Macedonia United Methodist Church is located on Riley Roberts Road in Dames Quarter. This African American church was established November 11, 1865. The church records are unclear about its establishment but do name several original members: George White, George F. Fields, Frank Dashield, and Henry A. Jones were among those present at the time. Macedonia United Methodist Church's appearance has changed very little over the years. The handicap ramp was added on July 21, 1997. The congregation is a small one now, as are many other churches. (Courtesy John F. Jones Jr.)

The school house on Riley Roberts Road in Dames Quarter was originally the elementary school for the African American children of the community. Grades one through six were taught in the school. After elementary school, the children went to Somerset School in Princess Anne. That building is now part of the University of Maryland Eastern Shore. After Integration, all elementary-aged children went to the Deal Island School. Head Start then occupied the building and was first supported by Somerset county from 1970 to 1991. From December 1991 until October 2004, Shore-Up administered the Head Start program. Now the building sits dormant, surrounded by high marsh grass and weeds. Eventually the marsh will take ownership, as it has with many other deserted structures. (Courtesy John Jones.)

CHAPTER 2

CHANCE

Chance was originally named Rock Creek. When the U.S. Post Office wanted to open a post office here, it decided the town had to be renamed. There was already a Rock Creek, Maryland, on the Western Shore, so the name could cause postal confusion. When told they were to have their own post office, the residents said "fat chance." Thus Chance became the name. (Edward "Tudor" Tarleton.)

Just beyond the marsh is a store. This photograph from 1957 shows Price's ESSO service station, a full-service gas station. The owner, Thomas "Bev" Price (left), is pictured in front of the door with a neighbor. Today there is no longer a full-service station in the area. This is now Lucky's Last Chance, a convenience store and grill. Here one can get that item forgotten at the grocery store in town, a sandwich, a pizza, or even a full meal. Pictured are David Alveberg (manager) and Rose Day (employee). It is the last place to gas up before reaching the end of the road. (Courtesy Thomas Price Jr.)

Rock Creek Church was the first organized church in the area. The original organization date is not recorded, but the second church was organized on March 3, 1807. It was located in the northeast corner of the Rock Creek Cemetery. The third church was built in 1875 in the center of the cemetery and was dedicated in 1876. Rock Creek Cemetery is still at the same place it was in 1807, when the second church was built. Many families still use it as their final resting place, and the church and its members maintain it carefully. (Courtesy William Wheatley.)

In 1900, the church at the cemetery burned, and the present Rock Creek Church was started. It was finished in 1901 on Deal Island Road. The Then photograph was taken in the 1950s. Rock Creek Methodist Church still stands on Deal Island Road. The photograph taken today shows the addition of a brick display announcing the times and days of services. (Courtesy Gordon Gladden.)

Rock Creek Church Hall is just west of the church on Deal Island Road. The building has been used for church suppers, meetings, and even for plays. There is a stage, and the floor slants slightly for better viewing of the stage. The kitchen has prepared many church suppers. Some time after the 1950s, an additional room was added to the church hall. This room has table games for the young people in the community to use. There is a youth meeting every week that welcomes children from all of the communities. (Courtesy Albert "Al" Brown.)

Directly across the road from Rock Creek Church was the Gladden's Country Store, pictured in the 1950s. Elbert W. Gladden was the owner. The building still stands as it has since the 1980s, when it closed for good. (Courtesy Gordon Gladden, son of Elbert W. Gladden.)

Elbert W. Gladden also grew strawberries in the fields on both sides of the store. Here he is plowing the field before planting his strawberry crop. Strawberries were a prominent crop in the area. Gladden also owned 12 skipjacks. A stand of lovely pine trees now fills what was once a field of strawberries. (Courtesy Gordon Gladden.)

Rock Creek Park borders Tangier Sound. This park was open area used for picnics and swimming. This postcard was part of the advertising campaign when it was decided to parcel the land and sell it for developing. Most of the residents living in Rock Creek Park are retirees. There are, however, some families that have lived here all their lives. (Author's collection.)

This unknown child is standing on the beach at Rock Creek Park. The beach was frequented by families for swimming and picnicking. There are no more beaches in Rock Creek Park. Riprap has been installed to prevent more erosion, and piers extend from each waterfront home. (Courtesy Thomas Price Jr.)

There were many beautiful large homes in Chance, and some are still there. This was the Shores family home, located in a beautiful remote area. All that is left of the beautiful home are a few crumbling walls and overgrowth where once was a beautiful yard. (Courtesy William Wheatley.)

This house stood on Haines Point Road in Chance and belonged to several generations of the Willing family. It was purposely burned in 1994 by Rev. Steve Willing when it became his. The home on the property now is lived in by Rev. Steve Willing, the great-great-grandson of the Willing family that owned the original house. (Courtesy Albert "Al" Brown.)

Over the years, there have been several bridges across Deal Island–Chance Harbor. This photograph shows the current bridge under construction above the older bridge in the 1980s. Now the entrance to the old bridge comes to an abrupt stop and looks as though it would drop into the harbor. (Courtesy Fay Hoffman Pianka.)

During the 1950s, when this photograph was taken, there were many skipjacks in Deal Island–Chance Harbor. Today there may be one or two skipjacks tied up to unload the daily catch. This photograph was taken from the Chance side of the harbor. (Courtesy Jay Harford.)

The old Deal Island Bridge can be seen in the distance beyond the skipjacks and other boats. In the center, what appears to be a box in the water is a soft crab shedding float. The new bridge is higher, longer, and much easier to see now that there is not any business taking place between the shore and the bridge. (Courtesy Charles "Tommy" Northam.)

Scott's Cove Marina in Chance is owned and operated by the Willing family. In the late 1950s (either 1958 or 1959), the first basin was developed after a canal had been dug to provide access from the harbor. Prior to this, the Willing family had a marina at another location in Chance for two generations. The marina now has two basins with 60 slips, a boat ramp, boat-lifting equipment, and a repair shop. Repair of all types of boats is available here. (Courtesy Shirley Willing Massey.)

Prior to boat lifts, boats were lifted out of the water with a railway. If one looks closely, the rail can be seen beneath the side of this skipjack. Today boat lifts are used, but repairs to a skipjack are done basically the same way they were years ago. This is the *Ida May* in Scott's Cove Marina being refitted by her owners, Elbert and Gordon Gladden. (Courtesy Albert "Al" Brown.)

CHANCE

Most if not all of these men were captains of skipjacks. From left to right are (first row) P. Walter, J. Webster, L. Anderson III, W. Webster, J. Bennett, W. Tankersley, E. Kelly, E. Collier, J. Ford, and A. Brown; (second row) J. Tankersley, G. Gibson, T. Kelley, unidentified, S. Allen, unidentified, and T. Webster. Standing in back wearing a derby is W. Shores. Today there are three licensed skipjack captains on Deal Island. They are, from left to right, Delmas Benton of the *Fannie Daugherty*, Arthur Daniels of the *City of Crisfield*, and Walton Benton of the *Somerset*. There are only five skipjack captains licensed to dredge oysters on the Chesapeake Bay. (Courtesy Albert "Al" Brown.)

Many skipjacks called Deal Island home. These are a few in the harbor. Today, three of the five skipjacks licensed to oyster on the Chesapeake Bay berth here. This photograph was taken at Scott's Cove Marina as the boats are readied for the annual Labor Day Skipjack Race. From left to right, they are the *Fannie Daugherty*, built in 1904, the *City of Crisfield*, built in 1949, and the *Somerset*, built in 1949. (Courtesy Gordon Gladden.)

CHAPTER 3

DEAL ISLAND

Legend tells of some survivors of a shipwreck being stranded on the island and naming it Devil's Island. After several years, a minister renamed it Diel's Island, the Greek word for devil. In time, Diel's became Deal's, and the U.S. Post Office dropped the "s" to make it Deal Island, as it is today. Because Tangier Sound is shallow, a very long pier was built from the island into the sound to accommodate vessels that traveled the Chesapeake Bay. Several of the buildings seen in the distance no longer exist. (Courtesy Charles "Tommy" Northam.)

The bridge crossing the harbor during the 1950s was made of wood with wooden railings. Today the bridge is surfaced with concrete and asphalt with concrete jersey walls for railings. The bridge is also much steeper to allow more room underneath for boats to pass. (Courtesy Charles "Tommy" Northam.)

The photograph above shows Deal Island Road coming from the old bridge. Today part of the old road can be seen to the right of the sign welcoming visitors to Deal Island, Home of the Skipjacks. The road now is to the left of this welcoming piece of landscaping. (Courtesy Fay Hoffman Pianka.)

After crossing the bridge, turn right at the first road to enter the harbor. This is Anderson's Store, where fishing needs and gas could be purchased. The store still stands and has been operated by a couple of different people over the years. At the time of this writing, it is not in operation. (Courtesy Albert "Al" Brown.)

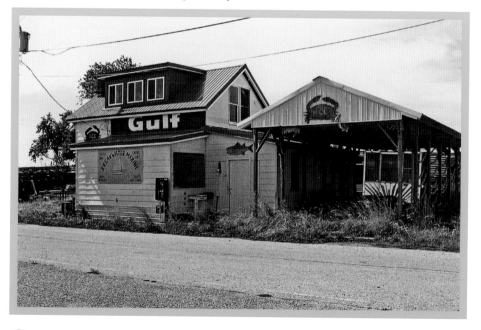

The earlier view (below) is from the west side of the harbor. The bridge is in the distance, as are skipjacks and some powerboats. From approximately the same location now, the bridge can be seen, but no boats are anchored in the harbor anymore. The oyster boats bring their catch to this part of the harbor for one of the seafood distributors to buy. (Courtesy Gordon Gladden.)

The view below is from the bridge looking down on the west side of the harbor. There are two skipjacks docked and several powerboats. From about the same part of the bridge, the view is quite different today. There are some powerboats in slips, and DNR's boat docks here. In the background is the Deal Island Seafood building. Crabs, both hard-shelled and soft-shelled, are sold here. There are also soft crab shedding floats. (Courtesy of Charles "Tommy" Northam.)

Brown and Anderson Fishing Parties was a good place to get a reservation to go fishing. An owner of the Anderson Hotel was one of the partners in this business. This large building still belongs to a member of the Anderson family. It replaces the old building and houses soft crab shedding floats. Soft crabs are a popular product of the area. (Courtesy Thomas Price Jr.)

In this earlier view of Deal Island–Chance Harbor from the grounds of the harbor facing west, there are many boats, both skipjacks and powerboats. The photograph below has been taken from the same area in the harbor. There aren't as many boats, and they all are powerboats. There are no skipjacks in this harbor. Occasionally one will be docked near an area where oysters are unloaded. (Courtesy Gordon Gladden.)

Brown's service station was located on the south side of Deal Island Road just west of Hotel Road. Later it was owned be the Harrison family. It burned to the ground in September 1952. The boy on the pony is Thomas B. Price Sr., who later owned the service station in Chance. Today there is a family home where the service station once stood. (Courtesy Albert "Al" Brown.)

Capt. Johnnie Bennett's barn was on the north side of Deal Island Road just west of Hotel Road. In the earlier photograph, the building looks as though it has already been deserted. Many of the old homes on Hotel Road are still there, but like so many of the buildings, the barn on the corner is gone. (Courtesy Charles "Tommy" Northam.)

The Anderson Hotel sat at the end of Hotel Road. Business people and tourists would stay at the hotel. Many came to hunt and fish. It could accommodate 85 people in the main building and two smaller buildings. Most of the hotel was damaged by a storm in August 1933. As near as can be determined, this private home may be in the approximate location of the hotel. It is very hard to say, because much of the land has eroded. The hotel may actually have been farther into Tangier Sound. (Courtesy Albert "Al" Brown.)

Steamboats were the main means of travel to and from the area. The steamboats would bring needed products and passengers to the wharf at the end of Hotel Road. They also carried passengers and products being shipped to market, including strawberries, tomatoes, and other farmed items, as well as whatever seafood was in season: soft crabs, hard crabs, oysters, and so forth. Hotel Road now comes to an abrupt stop. There is only riprap and the memories of the steamboat days. (Edward "Tudor" Tarleton.)

The Anderson Hotel had two small buildings to accommodate guests when the main building was full. These buildings were located very near the hotel. Today, there is nothing to remind one of their existence. Only high marsh grass and telephone wires occupy the area. (Courtesy Albert "Al" Brown.)

Johnnie's Place, owned and operated by John Bennett, was a store, which also operated a taxicab service for the island. This was a place where the gentlemen would get together. Like other buildings on Hotel Road, there is nothing in its place now but high marsh grass and telephone wires—and, of course, the memories of Johnnie's Place. (Courtesy Albert "Al" Brown.)

JOHNNIE'S PLACE AND TAXI SERVICE — PHONE 2911
DEAL ISLAND, MD.

When this earlier photograph was taken, people bought ice for iceboxes and for keeping seafood cold. The icehouse also served as the first source of electricity to the area. Again the buildings are gone. There was more land that has eroded over time and has been shored up with riprap. (Melvin White.)

The sign over the door announces the Deal Island Bank, a branch of the Bank of Somerset that was started in 1908. It closed during the Depression era in the 1930s. It also housed a switchboard for the telephone company in the area. The bank building appears to be as sound as it ever was. It sits empty now. (Courtesy Albert "Al" Brown.)

This building was the barbershop. It was located on Deal Island Road very near the firehouse. The barbershop is still there but has a stack of wood sitting beside the firehouse. Some gentlemen wish it was still there—now the nearest barbershop is in Princess Anne, nearly 15 miles away. (Courtesy Albert "Al" Brown.)

Established in 1879, St. John's Methodist Church is on Deal Island Road. It is a large church with tin paneling on the walls and ceilings, lovely stained glass windows, and a cemetery that surrounds the church. Today St. John's Methodist Church is still a very active part of the community. Its appearance hasn't changed over the years except for the dark roofs. (Courtesy Edward "Tudor" Tarleton.)

ST. JOHN'S, M.E. CHURCH, DEALS ISLAND, MD.

The Joshua Thomas Chapel sits on the grounds of St. John's Methodist Church. The chapel was used by the congregation prior to the building of the church. Rev. Joshua Thomas was in attendance when it was dedicated in 1850. He was the minister that brought the Methodist Church to the area. The chapel is still standing. Over the years, a new foundation was installed, and windows and siding, as well as the handicapped ramp, have been added. This chapel is probably the most important building here. To learn about Rev. Joshua Thomas, read *The Parson of the Islands*. (Courtesy Albert "Al" Brown.)

This picture postcard of a part of Deal Island shows a dirt road with several homes on it. There was once a country store on this part of the island too. The road is now blacktop, and most of the homes are gone. The one house in the photograph is also in the postcard. It has been maintained over the years and is lived in by a loving family. (Courtesy Gerald "Jerry" Thomas.)

This house on Deal Island Road is known as the Isabella House. It was built in 1875. The house is still in the same location. It is bright yellow with white trim. Most of the time, scaffoldings and ladders can be seen there, but no one is occupying the home now. (Courtesy Albert "Al" Brown.)

In 1962, a very bad storm hit the island. Some of the grave markers and caskets were lifted out of the ground because of the flooding. These graves are at John Wesley Methodist Church. The water table in the island is very high. For this reason, cement covers are placed on the graves, as they are in places like New Orleans to keep the graves from rising in storms. (Courtesy Fay Hoffman Pianka.)

The John Wesley Methodist Episcopal Church on Deal Island was an African American church on Deal Island Road. There was a large and active congregation when this photograph was taken. Today the church stands quiet and in need of repair. There are no Sunday services any more. Occasionally a funeral will bring activity to the church. (Courtesy Melvin White.)

This is not the first schoolhouse for Deal Island School. This building housed the school from 1940 until 1970. First through twelfth grades were taught here. The graduating classes were as small as four or five students. There was an occasional year when there would not be any students graduating. Today the Deal Island School is an elementary school with prekindergarten through fifth grade. The children are then taken by school bus to Westover for middle school and to Princess Anne for high school. The MAC program for senior citizens meets in the school and it is also the polling place on election days. (Courtesy Charles "Tommy" Northam.)

CHAPTER 4

WENONA

This is the Dewey H. Webster General Groceries Cash Store in Wenona. Fishing parties and supplies were to be found here as well as board lodging. Wenona is the last of the Deal Island communities, at the very end of Deal Island Road, but by boat, it is the first community. It is believed the name Wenona came from Native American name for the village originally here. (Courtesy Charles "Tommy" Northam.)

It was very common for the bridge crossing Wenona Creek to be flooded after heavy storms or in the fall when high tide, is very high. The bridge is higher now and the road surface has been raised to eliminate flooding as much as possible. The community was often stranded by the high tides or storms. A really strong storm such as a hurricane can still cause flooding. (Courtesy Charles "Tommy" Northam.)

This home belonged to a family named Northam and was built in 1911. It is on Deal Island Road in Wenona. The contributing photographer grew up in this house. The home is still standing at the same location. An addition has been added to the side of the house, and shutters adorn the windows. (Courtesy Charles "Tommy" Northam.)

Originally most of the houses were two stories high with four rooms. Some of the houses had additions built onto the back as this one did on Deal Island Road in Wenona. Several of the older homes, like this one, have been maintained, and their appearance is the same as it was many years ago. (Courtesy Charles "Tommy" Northam.)

The local blacksmith, Melvin Collier, and his family lived in this house on Deal Island Road. The smithy was in front of the house. It can no longer be seen. The house is still standing in the same place. Unfortunately, the lovely home is empty now and in disrepair. (Courtesy Albert "Al" Brown.)

The family of Albert Brown, a second-generation sailmaker, lived in this house on Deal Island Road in Wenona. The home has had a screened porch added and some updates made to the appearance. (Courtesy Albert "Al" Brown, grandson of the homeowner.)

During the 1950s, snowstorms were stronger and left heavy snow on the ground. This view of Deal Island Road in Wenona was taken shortly after a storm. Today the storms are not strong. Snow falls and disappears in just a few days, as it did the week the image below was taken. (Courtesy Charles "Tommy" Northam.)

St. Paul's Methodist Church was on the corner of Paul Benton Circle and Deal Island Road. It burned to the ground in 1982. A cemetery surrounded the church. The old cemetery, with a fence surrounding it, is still on that corner with a monument to the old church where it once stood. (Courtesy Albert "Al" Brown.)

This monument to St. Paul's was built to commemorate the location of the old church and depicts the church's appearance. The building of the new St. Paul's Methodist Church on the opposite side of Deal Island Road was completed in 1984. There is large meeting hall and a cemetery behind the church. The largest Methodist congregation attends here. (Courtesy Albert "Al" Brown.)

This was Wenona Harbor during the 1930s. The ground is covered with oyster shells, which were used to pave road surfaces. In the far rear is Little Deal Island. At that time, it could be inhabited and had a lodge on it. Now the harbor is much wider, and there are more buildings, a public boat ramp, and a blacktop parking lot. A powerboat with its oyster dredge and the mast of a skipjack (also outfitted for dredging) is visible. In the distance is Little Deal Island, which is no longer inhabited. (Courtesy Charles "Tommy" Northam.)

Shirley Webster White harvested soft crabs in this building on the south side of Wenona Harbor. The building has always been called "Shirley's Shack." The condition of the parking lot obscures the view. The old shack is still standing but no longer houses shedding soft crabs and is in need of repair. Items seem to have been just left around it. The parking lot is now blacktopped and provides a better view. (Courtesy Albert "Al" Brown.)

D. H. Webster's Store was near Wenona Harbor. Fishing needs as well as sandwiches and confections could be bought here. Today Arby's Store is in approximately the same location. The owner, Arby Holland, is a descendant of the Webster family that owned the original store. Arby's is the only store near the harbor today. (Courtesy Library of Congress, LC-USF34-040530-D.)

Vetra's Store was a general country store; there were many in the area. Some were right next door to one another. There is only the one store in Wenona now, Arby's (seen in an earlier photograph). Marsh grass hides the stacks of crab pots being stored here now. (Courtesy Charles "Tommy" Northam.)

Pictured in the 1930s, this party is comprised of a group of gentlemen preparing for a fun day fishing. They seem to be dressed quite formally by today's standards. Charter fishing is one of the ways folks here make their living. However, the boats are much larger, captains must be certified, and parties must be reserved in advance. (Courtesy Charles "Tommy" Northam.)

If one looks closely at this photograph, a skipjack can be seen sitting on land. It is on a railway, probably in need of some kind of repair. This was taken in the late 1940s or early 1950s. There are no more railways used for boat repair on Deal Island, and many of the buildings are no longer here. This is near the end of Deal Island Road. (Courtesy Charles "Tommy" Northam.)

This photograph, taken in May 1940, shows Edward T. (Eddie) Corbett at Wenona Harbor. Corbett was one of several fishermen photographed by Jack Delano that May. Corbett's grandson James "Jimmy" Corbett sits where his grandfather was sitting in 1940. The buildings are gone now. (Courtesy Library of Congress, LC-USF34-040529-D.)

Picking crabs or working in a packinghouse were jobs the ladies of the communities held. Crab picking is an art. Anyone can pick crabs, but to pick fast enough for a packinghouse was a definite skill. This building, photographed in the 1940s, could have been either a crab picking shed or a packinghouse. The shambled ruins are what is left of the building. No longer does anyone here work in a local crab packinghouse or cannery; they are gone now. (Courtesy Charles "Tommy" Northam.)

This photograph, taken May 1940, shows a long pier in Wenona Harbor for oyster and crab boats. Most of the boats were skipjacks in the 1940s. The harbor is a little different today. Most of the piers are shorter now and are used for fewer boats. The boats are larger and are mostly powerboats. (Courtesy Library of Congress call number, LC-USF34-040547-D.)

Albert E. Brown and Brother Sailmakers made sails by hand in this building for generations. Sailmaking was a skill and also an art. Sailing ships from up and down the Chesapeake came here for the best sails. However, sailmaking is no longer a viable business. After many years of service to the community and the sailing vessels of the Chesapeake, the business stopped and the building was torn down. This little white shed sits where masters once worked. (Courtesy Albert "Al" Brown.)

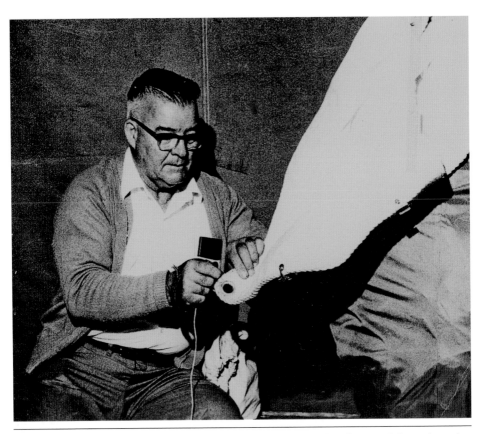

This photograph was taken by a visiting tourist and given to sailmaker Henry Brown, pictured making a sail. The sails were sewn by hand, which was very time consuming. Today there is a display in the Mariners Museum in Newport News, Virginia of the workbench and some of the tools used at the sail loft. (Then photograph courtesy Albert "Al" Brown, son of the sailmaker; now photograph courtesy Claudia Jew of the Mariners Museum.)

This May 1940 photograph shows crab floats. The floats were slats of wood spaced just far enough apart that a crab could not slide out. These floats were placed in the water for crabs to molt their hard shells and then were harvested for market. Crab floats are now out of the water in sheds or on wharfs. The water in the floats is kept moving and fresh. The soft crabs are harvested daily. (Courtesy Library of Congress, LC-USF34-040536-D.)

The very end of the island in Wenona is shown in May 1940 covered with oyster shells. Today a group of condominiums occupies the area. A blacktop road and yards fill the space once covered with oyster shells. (Courtesy Library of Congress, LC-USF34-040536-D.)

DEAL ISLAND/ CHANCE VFD

Pictured is the Deal Island/Chance Volunteer Fire Department (VFD) shield. The men and women of the Deal Island/Chance VFD answer calls of any type, from medical assistance to accidents and fires. When the alarm sounds, they respond, and that is why this book is for them. (Courtesy Benjamin "Benny" Bozman.)

The first firehouse was a converted store. It had one truck bay, which was all that was needed in 1954. The fire company was just starting and on very limited funds. A volunteer fire company depends on donations and grants to finance their needs. The firehouse now has five bays. The location is the same as it was in 1954, but the building has been extended to accommodate five vehicles. It is located on Deal Island Road about a half-mile west of the bridge. (Courtesy Benjamin "Benny" Bozman.)

In 1954, when the fire company was started, a used pumper truck was purchased. This was the first and, for a time, the only fire truck they had. She was named "Nellie Belle" with affection for her service. Today there are five service vehicles. They are a 1976 GMC/Pierce engine, 1988 GMC pumper/tanker, 1999 Pierce Saber, 2005 Ford brush truck with skid package, and an ambulance. (Courtesy Benjamin "Benny" Bozman.)

The first firefighting training class in 1954 included, from left to right, (first row) Earl Webster, Oscar "Dipper" Abbott, Jack Webster, Roger "Pip" Abbott, and William "Cud" Webster; (second row) Preston "Wicky" Wheatley, Edward "Blue" Webster, Kenneth Webster, Gene "Tuney" Webster, and Edward "Tudor" Tarleton; (third row) Fred Henderson, Robert France, Phil Price, Eldridge France, Elbert Gladden, William Shores, and Bennett Webster; (fourth row) Stanford Jones, Lee Webster, Danny Ray Benton, Charles "Stoney" Whitelock Sr., Harry Walters, Kirwin Abbott, and William Waters. Not photographed are Harry "Sonny" Abbott and Carroll Walters. The most recent photograph of the fire fighters was taken at the 2008 Annual Banquet. The force is much larger then it was in 1954 and includes women and a cadet training group. (Courtesy Benjamin "Benny" Bozman.)

The first new truck purchased by the fire company was the GMC pumper shown here. The latest addition to the fleet is a 23-foot Sea Ox with a 25-horsepower Mercury outboard engine that can reach a speed of 30 knots. This was donated by St. Michael's Fire Department. It has been completely revamped with the latest in electronics and other equipment. Marine 4 was launched on Labor Day 2007 at the Annual Skipjack Race. (Courtesy Charles "Tommy" Northam.)

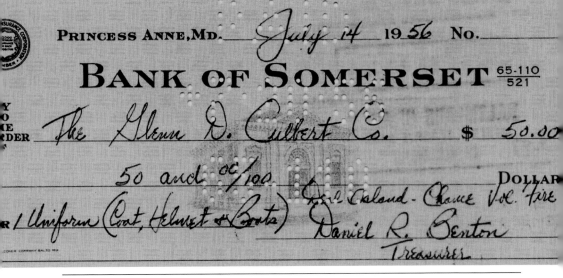

PRINCESS ANNE, MD. _July 14_ 19 56 No. _____

BANK OF SOMERSET 65-110/521

PAY TO THE ORDER _The Glenn D. Culbert Co._ $ _50.00_

50 and 00/100 _____ DOLLARS

FOR _1 Uniform (Coat, Helmet & Boots)_

Deal Island - Chance Vol. Fire
Daniel R. Benton
Treasurer

This is an actual cancelled $50 check written in 1956 to purchase a set of turnout gear for the Deal Island/Chance VFD. The turnout gear consisted of boots, a coat, and a helmet. This quote from a supplier of fire equipment itemizes the cost of a set of turnout gear today. Firemen are required to have more gear than in 1956, and the cost has increased in 53 years. (Then photograph courtesy Benjamin "Benny" Bozman; now photograph courtesy Daniel " Danny Ray" Webster.)

Scott Ward, Regional Sales Representative
10228 Governor Lane Blvd. Suite 3010 Williamsport, MD 21795
Toll Free Ph. 800-296-3473 / Mobile 443-783-3636 / Fax 410-968-0763 / EMAIL scottward@mesfire.com

CONFIDENTIAL PRICE QUOTATION

CUSTOMER:	DATE:	PRICE QUOTATION NUMBER:
Deal Island Fire Company	2-20-2009	NOW!
Attn: Danny Webster	YOUR INQUIRY DATE: 2-20-2009	SPECIAL INSTRUCTIONS: FAX TO: 410-784-2196
	ESTIMATED DELIVERY: 3-4 Weeks ARO	TO BE SHIPPED VIA: Best Way
QUOTE GOOD FOR: 30 DAYS	SALES REPRESENTATIVE: Scott Ward	TERMS NET 30 / WHO PAYS FREIGHT? CUSTOMER PAYS

PRICE QUOTATION OUTLINED BELOW, SUBJECT TO THE FOLLOWING CONDITIONS:

The prices and terms on this quotation are not subject to verbal changes or other agreements unless approved in writing by the Home Office of the Seller. All quotations and agreements are contingent upon strikes, accidents, fires, availability of materials and all other causes beyond our control. Prices are based on costs and conditions existing on date of quotation and are subject to change by the Seller before final acceptance. Typographical and stenographic errors are subject to correction. Purchaser agrees to accept either overage or shortage not in excess of ten percent to be charges for pro-rata. Purchaser assumes liability for patent and copyright infringement when goods are made to Purchaser's specifications. When quotation specifies material to be furnished by the purchaser, ample allowance must be made for reasonable spoilage and material must be of suitable quality to facilitate efficient production. Conditions not specifically stated herein shall be governed by established trade customs. Terms inconsistent with those stated herein, which may appear on Purchaser's formal order, will not be binding on the Seller.

**Shipping & Handling Charges apply unless otherwise noted.**

QTY	Part #	PRODUCT DESCRIPTION	PRICE	AMOUNT
1.00	COAT	GLOBE NOMEX TURNOUT COAT	$ 800.00	$ 800.00
1.00	PANTS	GLOBE NOMEX TURNOUT PANTS	$ 700.00	$ 700.00
1.00	BOOTS	RANGER RUBBER BUNKER BOOTS	$ 150.00	$ 150.00
1.00	HOOD	AMERICAN FIREWEAR NOMEX HOOD	$ 35.00	$ 35.00
1.00	GLOVES	AMERICAN FIREWEAR FIREFIGHTING GLOVES	$ 55.00	$ 55.00
1.00	HELMET	MORNING PRIDE STRUCTURAL FIRE HELMET	$ 260.00	$ 260.00
		TOTAL TO OUTFIT A FIREFIGHTER		$ 2,000.00

This 1942 Ford fire truck handled the first fire the Deal Island/Chance Volunteer Fire Department had to fight. It was in Wenona at the home of Price Webster. Oddly enough, the young man that started the fire now lives there. Today the Deal Island/Chance Volunteer Fire Department answers the call for medical assistance and controlled burns as well as any fire in the communities they protect. This photograph was taken at a control burn, which is when a resident has a structure or other combustible articles they own burned. The firemen do the burn in order to keep it contained and to prevent a fire from spreading. (Then photograph courtesy Charles "Tommy" Northam; now photograph courtesy Daniel "Dan" Will.)

ACROSS AMERICA, PEOPLE ARE DISCOVERING SOMETHING WONDERFUL. *THEIR HERITAGE.*

Arcadia Publishing is the leading local history publisher in the United States. With more than 3,000 titles in print and hundreds of new titles released every year, Arcadia has extensive specialized experience chronicling the history of communities and celebrating America's hidden stories, bringing to life the people, places, and events from the past. To discover the history of other communities across the nation, please visit:

www.arcadiapublishing.com

Customized search tools allow you to find regional history books about the town where you grew up, the cities where your friends and family live, the town where your parents met, or even that retirement spot you've been dreaming about.